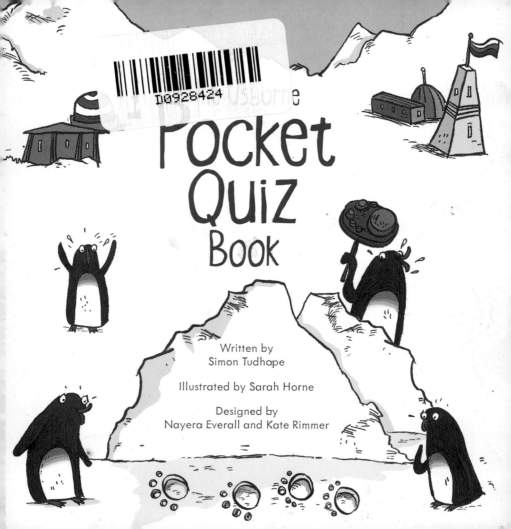

# Usborne
# Pocket
# Quiz
# Book

Written by
Simon Tudhope

Illustrated by Sarah Horne

Designed by
Nayera Everall and Kate Rimmer

1. **In the legends, what was the name of King Arthur's castle?**
   a) Windsor   b) Hogwarts   c) Camelot

2. **What is a 40-40 score called in tennis?**
   a) evens   b) draw   c) deuce

3. **Which gas is put in balloons to make them float?**
   a) oxygen
   b) helium
   c) carbon dioxide

4. **The Mona Lisa was painted by Vincent van Gogh.**
   True or false?

5. **How many teeth do elephants use to chew their food?**
   a) 4   b) 32   c) 56

**6** Which of these is a nickname for a giraffe?
a) stench pig
b) reek hog
c) stink bull

**7** Where can you see the ruins of ancient Aztec pyramids?
a) Mexico   b) Wales   c) Russia

**8** Who was Al Capone?
a) pirate   b) gangster   c) cowboy

**9** What are the three particles in an atom? Protons, neutrons and...
a) robotons   b) klingons   c) electrons

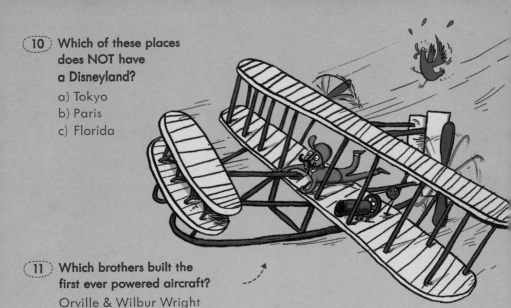

**10** Which of these places does NOT have a Disneyland?
a) Tokyo
b) Paris
c) Florida

**11** Which brothers built the first ever powered aircraft?
Orville & Wilbur Wright **or** Gary & Phil Neville?

**12** I begin my journey in the great lakes of central Africa, and make my way through jungles and deserts, before finally reaching the Mediterranean Sea.
Which river am I?

**13** What does a skunk's spray smell most like?
a) rotten eggs and rancid milk
b) burning rubber and urine
c) dog mess and sweat

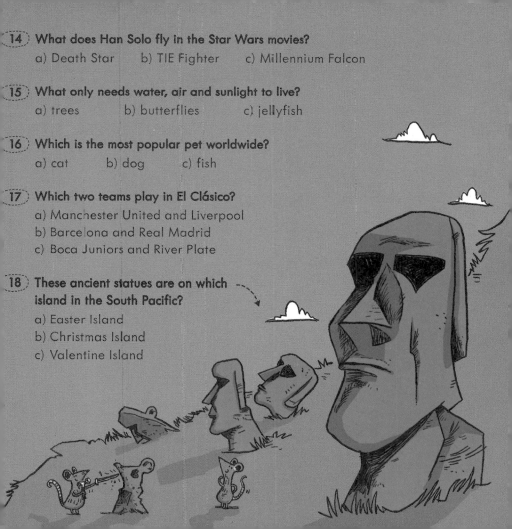

**14** What does Han Solo fly in the Star Wars movies?
   a) Death Star    b) TIE Fighter    c) Millennium Falcon

**15** What only needs water, air and sunlight to live?
   a) trees    b) butterflies    c) jellyfish

**16** Which is the most popular pet worldwide?
   a) cat    b) dog    c) fish

**17** Which two teams play in El Clásico?
   a) Manchester United and Liverpool
   b) Barcelona and Real Madrid
   c) Boca Juniors and River Plate

**18** These ancient statues are on which island in the South Pacific?
   a) Easter Island
   b) Christmas Island
   c) Valentine Island

**19** How was Queen Marie Antoinette executed during the French Revolution:

a) hangman   b) guillotine   c) bagatelle

**20** Where would you find manga?

a) in a circus
b) in a fruit market
c) in a comic book store

**21** Which dogs pull snow sleds?

a) poodles
b) huskies
c) bloodhounds

**22** What makes up 70% of the human body?

a) carbon
b) water
c) calcium

**23** Match a word on the left and right to make the names of three baseball teams.

a) New York      1) Red Sox

b) Los Angeles   2) Yankees

c) Boston        3) Dodgers

**24** In *The Muppet Show*, who is Miss Piggy in love with?

a) Rizzo the rat

b) The Great Gonzo

c) Kermit the frog

**25** Which monster could turn into a bat?

a) Medusa

b) banshee

c) Dracula

**26** What are these boats in Hong Kong called?

a) junks

b) tugboats

c) catamarans

**27** What's the biggest planet in the Solar System?

    a) Uranus         b) Jupiter         c) Saturn

**28** What are baby porcupines called?

    a) porcupups         b) porcupops         c) porcupettes

**29** Who said 'open sesame!' to enter a secret cave filled with treasure?

    a) Ali Baba         b) Pinocchio         c) Merlin

**30** Which drink is best for keeping bones and teeth strong?

    a) lemonade         b) milk         c) coffee

**31** If you traced around a map of Italy's coastline, what would your picture look like?

a) tennis racket    b) starfish    c) boot

**32** What is the record age for a giant tortoise?

a) 55 years old
b) 155 years old
c) 255 years old

**33** In space, can anyone hear you scream?

*Arghhh*

**34** What did dinosaurs never eat?

a) eggs
b) rabbits
c) fish

**35** Who was a Native American war chief?

a) Buffalo Bill
b) Wily Coyote
c) Crazy Horse

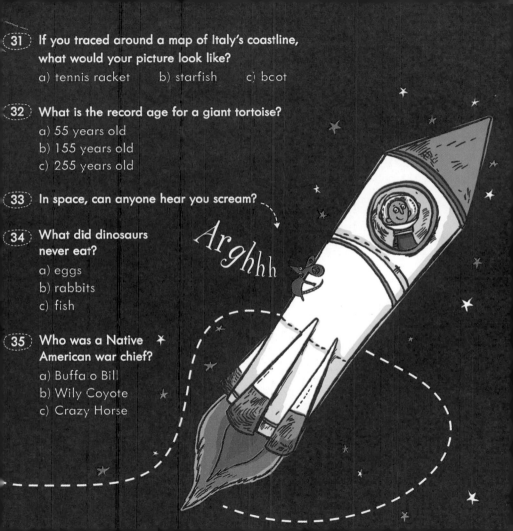

**36** How long does it take the Earth to go around the Sun?
  a) 1 day    b) 1 month    c) 1 year

**37** How should you deal with a charging rhino?
  a) keep quiet and throw a rock to one side
  b) shout and scream as loudly as you can
  c) punch it on the nose

**38** Scientists who study dinosaur fossils are called:
  a) dinosaurologists
  b) paleontologists
  c) archaeologists

**39** Where would you be if you saw these Masai women?
  a) Kenya
  b) Argentina
  c) Japan

**40** In which sport can you win the Stanley Cup?
  a) American football
  b) ice hockey
  c) baseball

**41** Which brothers made the first hot-air balloon, over 100 years before planes were invented?

  a) Montgolfier
  b) Grimm
  c) Jackson

**42** Which bird plucks monkeys out of the trees to eat?

  a) king vulture
  b) fearful owl
  c) harpy eagle

**43** In *Alice's Adventures in Wonderland*, who was at the Mad Hatter's tea party?

  a) The Cheshire Cat
  b) The Queen of Hearts
  c) The March Hare

**44** We sailed in longships.
We loved fighting and feasting.
We were the terror of northern Europe.

Who are we?

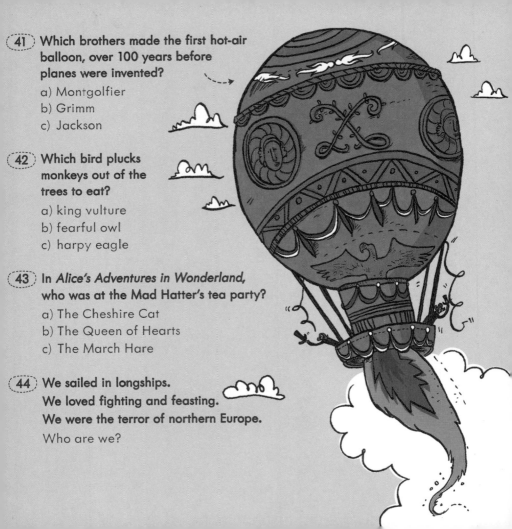

**45)** Which race takes place over three weeks, covers over 3,600km (2,200 miles) and finishes in Paris?

a) Tour de France
b) Monaco Grand Prix
c) Cheltenham Gold Cup

**46)** Where do people eat their food with chopsticks?

a) India   b) Argentina   c) China

**47)** What are a meerkat's greatest enemies?

a) birds of prey
b) jackals
c) snakes

**48)** What present does Santa give the boy in *The Snowman*?

a) a toy dog
b) a scarf
c) a lump of coal

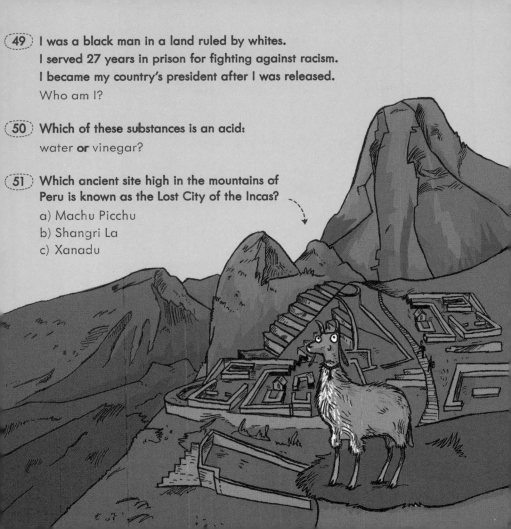

**49** I was a black man in a land ruled by whites.
I served 27 years in prison for fighting against racism.
I became my country's president after I was released.
Who am I?

**50** Which of these substances is an acid:
water **or** vinegar?

**51** Which ancient site high in the mountains of
Peru is known as the Lost City of the Incas?
a) Machu Picchu
b) Shangri La
c) Xanadu

**52** What is the main gas in air?

  a) helium    b) oxygen    c) nitrogen

**53** Which of these is not one of the
12 animals in the Chinese zodiac?

  a) rat    b) monkey    c) penguin

**54** What flag does a surrendering army fly?

  a) a white flag
  b) a black flag
  c) a yellow flag

**55** What is the nickname for the
South Africa rugby team?

  a) Wallabies
  b) Springboks
  c) All Blacks

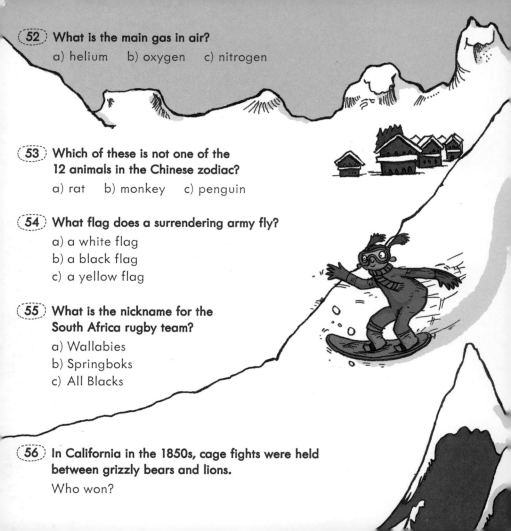

**56** In California in the 1850s, cage fights were held
between grizzly bears and lions.

  Who won?

**57** Where are the Alps? ---→
  a) Europe
  b) Australia
  c) South America

**58** What is Turkish delight?
  a) a sweet snack
  b) a hot bath
  c) a red flower

**59** In the Second World War, the Nazis held troublesome prisoners-of-war in a maximum-security stone castle. Was its name:

Warmitz **or** Colditz?

**60** What did the ancient Romans use to clean themselves?
  a) olive oil    b) wine    c) soap

**61** How did Hansel and Gretel beat the wicked witch?
  a) they trapped her in a cupboard
  b) they pushed her down a well
  c) they shoved her into an oven

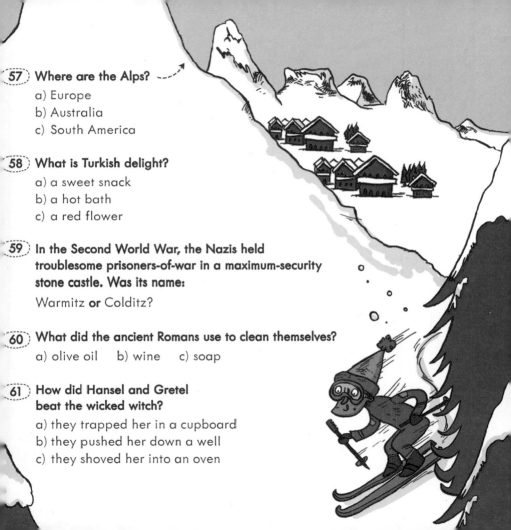

(62) **Where can you go swimming with dolphins?**
a) Caribbean Sea  b) Baltic Sea  c) North Sea

(63) **What destroyed central London in 1666?**
a) fire  b) earthquake  c) flood

(64) **Which river did Huckleberry Finn sail down?**
a) Colorado
b) Rio Grande
c) Mississippi

(65) **Which is the hardest substance?**
a) iron
b) diamond
c) wood

**66** Which three countries are in Europe?

a) Bolivia　b) Austria　c) Denmark　d) Algeria　e) Latvia

**67** In Greek mythology, the Minotaur had the head of a viper.
True or false?

**68** I am a giant gas planet...
...with a great red spot.
I am over a thousand times larger than Earth.
What am I?

**69** What traditional Russian instrument looks like a triangular guitar?

a) mandolin
b) balalaika
c) hurdy gurdy

**70** Which big cat lives in the Amazon rainforest?

a) leopard
b) jaguar
c) tiger

**71** How many Earths would fit inside the Sun?

a) one thousand    b) one million    c) one billion

**72** Which snakes are normally used by snake charmers?

a) adders    b) mambas    c) cobras

**73** What is Scrooge's first name in *A Christmas Carol*?

a) Ebenezer    b) Archibald    c) Jeremiah

**74** Who was killed by an arrow through the eye at the Battle of Hastings?

a) William the Conqueror
b) Edward the Confessor
c) Harold II

**75** What language do people speak in Brazil:

Spanish **or** Portuguese?

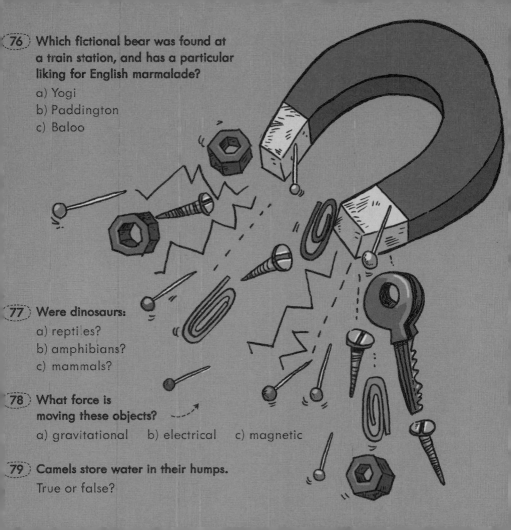

**76** Which fictional bear was found at a train station, and has a particular liking for English marmalade?
a) Yogi
b) Paddington
c) Baloo

**77** Were dinosaurs:
a) reptiles?
b) amphibians?
c) mammals?

**78** What force is moving these objects?
a) gravitational   b) electrical   c) magnetic

**79** Camels store water in their humps. True or false?

**80** I was the largest and most luxurious ship ever built.
They called me 'unsinkable'...
...but I was sunk by an iceberg on my first voyage.
What am I?

**81** How many atoms fit on the head of a pin?
a) 5 thousand
b) 5 million
c) 5 trillion

**82** A vampire bat's diet consists entirely of blood.
True or false?

**83** What's the nickname for ankylosaurs?
a) tank dinosaurs
b) demon dinosaurs
c) punk dinosaurs

**84** **Which is bigger:**
the Sun **or** the planet Jupiter?

**85** **In *Beauty and the Beast*, why did the fairy turn the prince into a beast?**
a) he refused her shelter from a storm
b) he cut down her woodland home
c) he refused to marry her

**86** **Where is Neuschwanstein Castle?**
a) Germany
b) France
c) Spain

**87** **What sport did Babe Ruth play?**
a) tennis    b) baseball    c) ice hockey

**88** **What is America's capital city?**
a) Washington DC    b) Chicago    c) New York

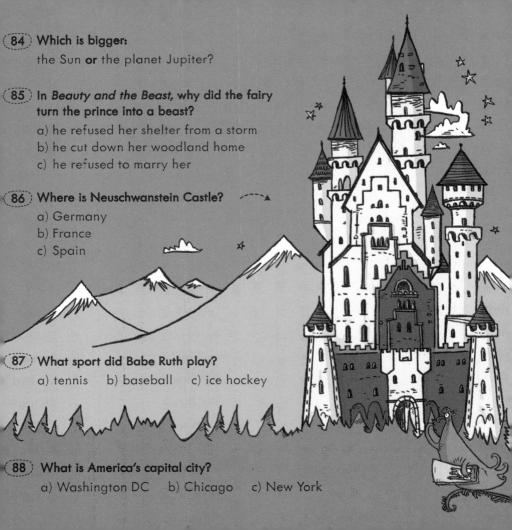

**89** Which of these is NOT one of Santa's reindeer?
   a) Dasher    b) Blitzen    c) Ranger

**90** Where did the Yellow Brick Road lead?
   a) the Emerald City
   b) Neverland
   c) Rivendell

**91** I was the terror of the seven seas.
   I had a long, dark beard.
   My real name was Edward Teach.
   Who am I?

**92** On average, how many people
   are eaten by crocodiles each year?
   a) 100    b) 1,000    c) 5,000

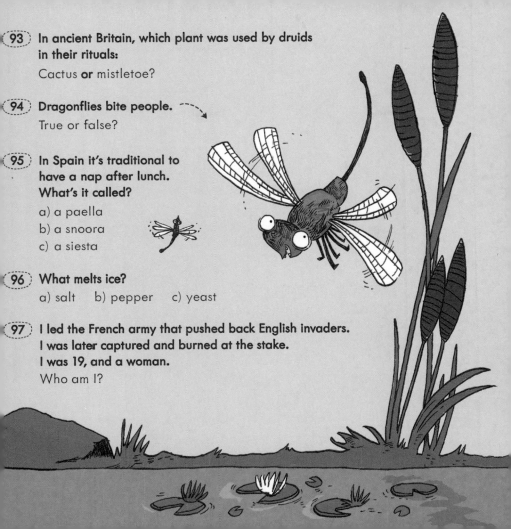

**93** In ancient Britain, which plant was used by druids in their rituals:

Cactus **or** mistletoe?

**94** Dragonflies bite people.
True or false?

**95** In Spain it's traditional to have a nap after lunch. What's it called?
a) a paella
b) a snoora
c) a siesta

**96** What melts ice?
a) salt    b) pepper    c) yeast

**97** I led the French army that pushed back English invaders. I was later captured and burned at the stake. I was 19, and a woman.
Who am I?

**98** What ships did Vikings sail in?
a) galleons
b) kayaks
c) longships

**99** What causes colds: viruses **or** bacteria?

**100** What's the platform number for the *Hogwarts Express* from King's Cross Station?
a) 4 ½   b) 7 ⅔   c) 9 ¾

**101** Would you ever see a polar bear eating a penguin in the wild?

**102** Which mythical creature guarded an ancient Greek city by asking visitors a riddle, and eating those who got the answer wrong?
a) an ogre   b) a sphinx   c) a dragon

**103** Which element is used to make atomic bombs: potassium **or** uranium?

**104** In the Middle Ages, were sheep five times smaller or five times larger than they are today?

**105** What are baby sharks called?
a) pups    b) kids    c) sharklets

**106** Match the name with their superhero.
a) Peter Parker         1) Superman
b) Clark Kent           2) Batman
c) Bruce Wayne          3) Spiderman

**107** Moroccan stews are cooked and served in an earthenware pot called a:
a) wok
b) tagine
c) balti

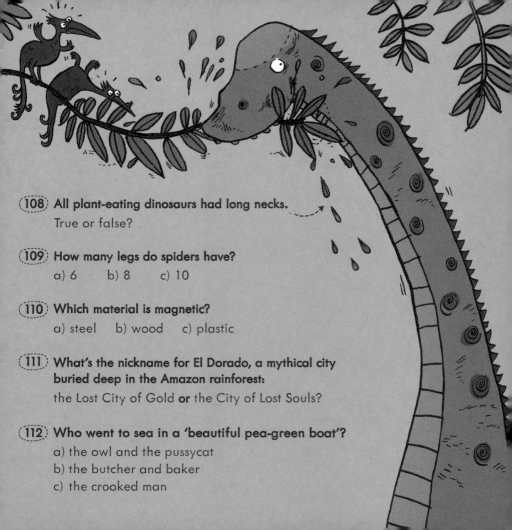

**108** All plant-eating dinosaurs had long necks.
True or false?

**109** How many legs do spiders have?
a) 6  b) 8  c) 10

**110** Which material is magnetic?
a) steel  b) wood  c) plastic

**111** What's the nickname for El Dorado, a mythical city
buried deep in the Amazon rainforest:
the Lost City of Gold **or** the City of Lost Souls?

**112** Who went to sea in a 'beautiful pea-green boat'?
a) the owl and the pussycat
b) the butcher and baker
c) the crooked man

**113** Is the bushy hair on a male lion's head called:

a mane **or** a mullet?

**114** What type of boat is taking these people down the Mississippi river?

a) tugboat
b) galleon
c) paddle steamer

**115** Do camels in the Sahara desert have one hump or two?

**116** How was the King of England, Charles I, executed in 1649?

a) hanged b) shot c) beheaded

**117** Which of these is NOT a horse race?

a) Kentucky Derby
b) Grand National
c) Dakar Rally

**118** In the Asterix books, what does Obelix like to eat most?
   a) cheese   b) chicken   c) wild boar

**119** Which bad-tempered animal has a hide that's so thick it's almost bulletproof?
   a) hippo   b) buffalo   c) tiger

**120** How far is it between Alaska in North America and Russia in Asia?
   a) 4km / 2.5 miles
   b) 400km / 250 miles
   c) 4,000km / 2,500 miles

**121** In the Middle Ages, which animals were often used by doctors:
   slugs **or** leeches?

**122** Which is the odd one out?
   a) Brazil
   b) Tokyo
   c) Sweden

**123** In the Middle Ages, which plague killed half the
people in Europe, and was spread by rat fleas?
a) Red Death    b) White Death    c) Black Death

**124** Which sport did Brian Lara play?
a) rugby    b) baseball    c) cricket

**125** Scientists have used genetic engineering
to bring Velociraptors back to life.
True or false?

**126** What underground demon almost killed
Gandalf in *The Lord of the Rings*?
a) Shelob    b) the Balrog    c) Smaug

**127** South of the Equator, water drains down a plughole in the opposite direction to north of the Equator.

True or false?

**128** Which animal has the most powerful bite in the world?

a) crocodile
b) grizzly bear
c) great white shark

**129** Who's the sea captain in the Tintin books?

a) Captain Cod
b) Captain Haddock
c) Captain Pollock

**130** What are these fighters called?

a) corsairs
b) bandits
c) gladiators

**131** Which superhero was not born on Earth?

a) The Incredible Hulk
b) Iron Man
c) Superman

**132** The air you breathe out contains more oxygen than the air you breathe in.
True or false?

**133** Who built the Colosseum?
a) Ancient Egyptians
b) Mongols
c) Romans

**134** Can a passenger plane survive being struck by lightning?

**135** I can turn my head nearly all the way around.
I see ten times better than humans at night.
I fly in almost total silence.
What am I?

**136** An adult human brain weighs the same as:
a) one can of beans
b) four cans of beans
c) ten cans of beans

**137** **What creature causes more human deaths than any other on the planet?**
  a) tiger
  b) king cobra
  c) mosquito

**138** **Match the money symbol to the country where that money is used:**
  a) €          1) Britain
  b) £          2) United States
  c) $          3) Germany

**139** **What was the name of King Arthur's sword?**
  a) Narsil    b) Heartsbane    c) Excalibur

**140** **Who was inside this coffin?**
  a) Abraham Lincoln
  b) Tutankhamun
  c) Genghis Khan

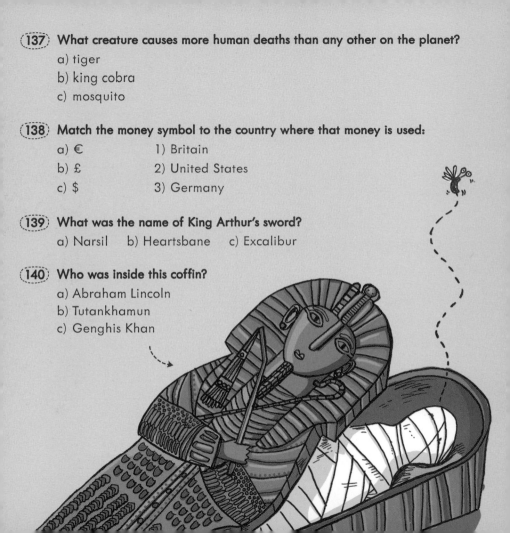

**141** Which is NOT a vegetable?
  a) pear
  b) carrot
  c) onion

**142** Who was the first woman
to fly solo across the Atlantic Ocean:
Amelia Earhart **or** Ellen MacArthur?

**143** What might have charged at other dinosaurs like a rhino:
Diplodocus **or** Triceratops?

**144** In the movie, what is E.T.'s disguise when he's smuggled
out of the house?
  a) old lady    b) ghost    c) raccoon

Is the biggest part of an iceberg
above the surface or below the surface?

**146** Which boxer bit a chunk out of his opponent's ear?
   a) Sugar Ray Leonard
   b) Mike Tyson
   c) Lennox Lewis

**147** What was Napoleon's last name?
   a) Bonaparte
   b) Blownapart
   c) Dynamite

**148** What is the highest mountain in Africa?
   a) The Matterhorn
   b) Mount Everest
   c) Kilimanjaro

**149** Was Robin Hood ever
King of England?

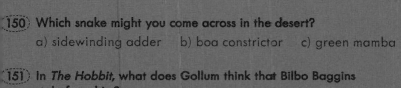

**150** Which snake might you come across in the desert?

    a) sidewinding adder    b) boa constrictor    c) green mamba

**151** In *The Hobbit,* what does Gollum think that Bilbo Baggins stole from him?

    a) a jewel    b) a ring    c) a sword

**152** Which has the greatest effect on the oceans' tides: the Sun **or** the Moon?

**153** Which hats are this Mexican - - - ➔ mariachi band wearing?

    a) stetsons
    b) sombreros
    c) tam o'shanters

**154** Which 20th-century war took place in the jungles of southeast Asia?

V _ _ _ _ _ m War

**155** Where can you see the Shaolin Monastery, where some of the world's best martial artists are trained?

a) Thailand
b) China
c) Japan

**156** How long were dinosaurs around for?

a) 165 thousand years
b) 165 million years
c) 165 billion years

**157** Pearls are found inside which animal's shell?

a) snail    b) crab    c) oyster

**158** Who is the movie hero Jack Sparrow?

a) a gladiator    b) a soldier    c) a pirate

**159** I love crackers and cheese and cups of tea.
I've been attacked by a criminal penguin and a robot dog.
I have a friend named Gromit.
Who am I?

**160** Which city was built first?
Rome **or** Las Vegas?

**161** What do climbers rub on their hands for extra grip?
a) olive oil    b) chalk    c) superglue

**162** Who were the Viking warriors with the most
fearsome reputation for bloodlust?
a) berserkers
b) marauders
c) immortals

**163** Identical twins have identical fingerprints.
True or false?

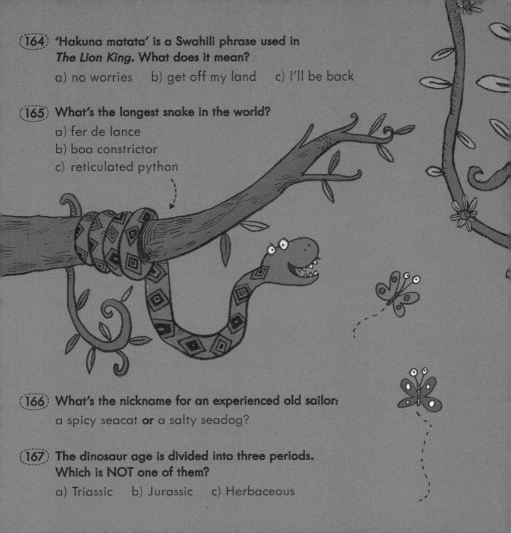

**164** 'Hakuna matata' is a Swahili phrase used in *The Lion King*. What does it mean?

a) no worries   b) get off my land   c) I'll be back

**165** What's the longest snake in the world?

a) fer de lance
b) boa constrictor
c) reticulated python

**166** What's the nickname for an experienced old sailor:

a spicy seacat **or** a salty seadog?

**167** The dinosaur age is divided into three periods. Which is NOT one of them?

a) Triassic   b) Jurassic   c) Herbaceous

**168** Which of these outlaws is a fictional character?
   a) Butch Cassidy
   b) The Sundance Kid
   c) The Lone Ranger

**169** What process do plants use to turn the Sun's energy into food?
   a) metamorphosis
   b) photosynthesis
   c) hypnosis

**170** What is a group of monkeys called?
   a) pack      b) tribe      c) troop

**171** Which storybook character flew from England to America in a giant peach carried by seagulls?
   a) James      b) Charlie      c) Matilda

**172** What was on the island of Alcatraz?
   a) maximum-security prison
   b) mental hospital
   c) monastery

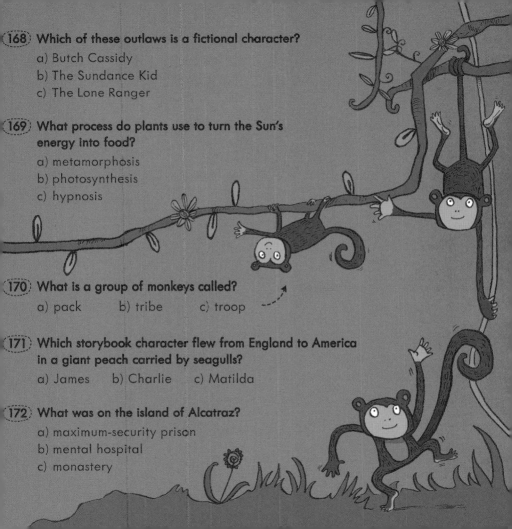

**173** What is the legendary ape that's said to walk on two legs and live in the forests of North America?

a) King Kong    b) Bigfoot    c) Yeti

**174** Where in London can you see waxwork replicas of famous people?

a) Houses of Parliament
b) Madame Tussauds
c) Tower of London

**175** In which sport can you score a maximum of 180?

a) darts    b) golf    c) pool

**176** Where's the Empire State Building?

a) Barcelona
b) Toronto
c) New York

ELIZABETH II

**177** Which of these animals were NOT around at the same time as the dinosaurs?

　　a) crocodiles　　b) sharks　　c) tigers

**178** In Cinderella, what did the Fairy Godmother turn into a golden carriage?

　　a) a mouse
　　b) a pumpkin
　　c) a mop and bucket

**179** In early Victorian times, chimney sweeps started work at what age?

　　a) 6　　b) 12　　c) 18

**180** The Sun is a star.
　　True or false?

**181** Which seahorses give birth?
   a) males
   b) females
   c) both

**182** What did Native Americans travel in:
   a) dinghies
   b) yachts
   c) canoes

**183** Which flag did pirates fly:
   the Jolly Roger **or** the Grumpy Codger?

**184** I fly with my umbrella...
   ...and my best friend is a chimney sweep.
   I think a spoonful of sugar helps the medicine go down.
   Who am I?

**185** Where did the Olympic Games first take place?

    a) ancient Egypt     b) ancient Greece     c) ancient Rome

**186** Which movie had two clownfish in starring roles?

    a) *The Little Mermaid*
    b) *Finding Nemo*
    c) *Shark's Tale*

**187** Who invented gunpowder?

    a) the Chinese
    b) the Aztecs
    c) the Romans

**188** What is a Tyrannosaurus rex most closely related to?

    a) cobra
    b) kangaroo
    c) chicken

**189** Which country lies on the Equator?

    a) Kenya     b) Canada     c) Greece

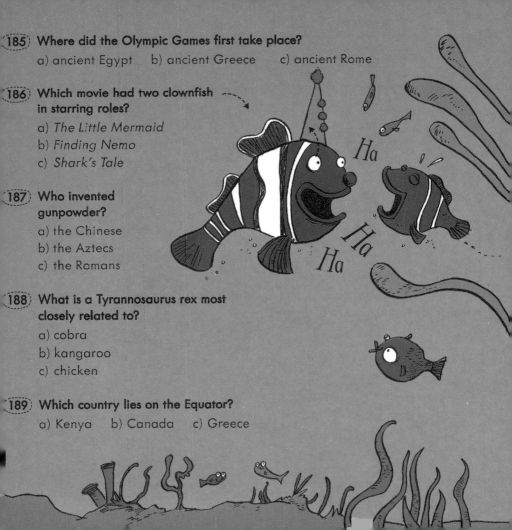

**190** The Great Barrier Reef is off the coast of Australia.
True or false?

**191** Which TV hero has a blue box that travels through time and space?
a) Doctor Who
b) Scooby Doo
c) Professor Xavier

**192** Which Barcelona player is the only person to have been named world player of the year four times?
a) Lionel Messi
b) Diego Maradona
c) Johan Cruyff

**193** When squirrels store nuts for the winter, do they bury them separately or in a large stash?

194. Which city had hanging gardens that were one of the seven wonders of the ancient world?
    a) Troy
    b) Atlantis
    c) Babylon

195. Which of these composers was deaf?
    a) Beethoven
    b) Wagner
    c) Mozart

196. Which animal hunts for salmon in summer?
    a) wolf
    b) beaver
    c) grizzly bear

197. Is Hollywood on the East or West coast of America?

198. In the story, who won the race between the hare and the tortoise?

**199** What is Kathmandu?
a) a type of boat
b) the capital of Nepal
c) a volcano near Hawaii

**200** Which is at the top of its food chain?
a) rabbit    b) carrot    c) fox

**201** Which movie hero has a green face, a yellow suit, and the catchphrase "Somebody stop me!"
a) The Mask
b) The Incredible Hulk
c) Wolverine

**202** This prehistoric sea creature is called Shonisaurus. Its eyeballs were as wide as...
a) saucers
b) large pizzas
c) car wheels

**203** After the First World War, which flower grew upon the old battlefields?
a) roses
b) poppies
c) tulips

**204** Who marched over the Alps mountain range with elephants in his army, to attack the Roman Empire?

a) Alexander the Great
b) Hannibal
c) Adolf Hitler

**205** I'm the most famous boxer of all time. I used to float like a butterfly... ...and sting like a bee. Who am I?

**206** Is the Loch Ness monster said to look like:

an ankylosaur
**or** a plesiosaur?

**207** If you sneezed in Germany, what would somebody say?

a) Schnitzel!
b) Lederhosen!
c) Gesundheit!

**208** Which dinosaur had the most powerful bite of any creature that has ever walked the Earth:

Tyrannosaurus rex **or** Velociraptor?

**209** Which of these is NOT a real element?
a) chlorine
b) argon
c) kryptonite

**210** Who had a flying carpet?
a) Ali Baba
b) Sinbad
c) Aladdin

**211** I am made of wood...
...but want to be a real boy.
My nose grows every time I tell a lie.
Who am I?

**212** Which planet is called 'the morning star' and 'the evening star' because it's seen in the sky at dawn and dusk?
a) Neptune    b) Venus    c) Uranus

**213** Who was the first man in space?
   a) Yuri Gagarin
   b) Neil Armstrong
   c) James T. Kirk

**214** What is a group of geese called?
   a) giggle
   b) gaggle
   c) goggle

**215** Who designed this strange ╌╌➤ church in Barcelona?
   Antoni Gaudí **or** Pablo Picasso?

**216** According to legend, who pulled the sword from the stone:
   Robin Hood **or** King Arthur?

**217** Are bacteria bigger or smaller than tadpoles?

**218** What was the Barbary Coast once famous for:
diamonds **or** pirates?

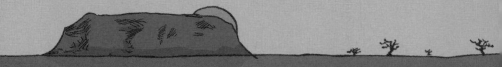

**219** Which sport is played at Wimbledon?
a) golf
b) tennis
c) basketball

**220** What dissolves
in water?
a) pepper
b) oil
c) salt

**221** Which country is home
of the didgeridoo?
a) Australia
b) Kenya
c) Brazil

**222** Did dinosaurs have bellybuttons?

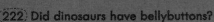

**223** What do caterpillars turn into?
a) butterflies
b) bees
c) toads

**224** I led the revolution against the British...
...but told my followers to use no violence.
I wore a white shawl and sandals.
Who am I?

**225** In *The Wizard of Oz*, what did
the Tin Man ask for?
a) a brain
b) a heart
c) courage

**226** What is $CO_2$?
a) carbon dioxide
b) hydrogen
c) oxygen

**227** What's the name of
this ancient fortification?
G _ _ _ _   _ _ _ _
of  C _ _ _ _

**228** Who made his last stand at the Battle of the Little Bighorn: General Custer **or** General Patton?

**229** Which galaxy are we in?
a) Andromeda   b) Whirlpool   c) Milky Way

**230** How many stars are there on the American flag?
a) 5   b) 20   c) 50

**231** In *Where the Wild Things Are*, what's still hot when Max gets home?
a) his bath
b) his supper
c) his bed

**232** What fish lures its prey with a bright light?
a) angler fish
b) vampire fish
c) trapdoor fish

**233)** What's the largest animal that's ever lived?

a) elephant    b) blue whale    c) Diplodocus

**234)** I was born from the death of a massive star.
I grow by sucking in everything around me.
Nothing can escape, not even light.
What am I?

**235)** Where is St. Basil's cathedral?

a) Scotland
b) China
c) Russia

**236)** My boss is M.
My colleague is Q.
My codename is 007.
Who am I?

**237)** Who came first:
Napoleon **or** Julius Caesar?

**(238) Where are the Pyramids of Giza?**
a) Saudi Arabia    b) Egypt    c) Pakistan

**(239) Which storybook hero was shipwrecked on a Caribbean island:**
Robinson Crusoe **or** Oliver Twist?

**(240) Roughly how long does it take your blood to circulate around your body?**
a) one second    b) one minute    c) one hour

**(241) I have a long neck and furry coat. I live in South America.**
**My name begins with the same two letters.**
What am I?

**242** **How did Ham the chimp make history in 1961?**
   a) He was the first ape to release a pop song.
   b) He was the first ape in space.
   c) He was the first ape to do long division.

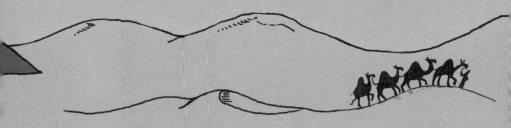

**243** **Which mysterious criminal terrorized the streets of London in the 1880s?**
   a) Jack the Ripper
   b) The Artful Dodger
   c) Professor Moriarty

**244** **Where can you find magma?**
   a) inside an atom
   b) inside a volcano
   c) inside a tree trunk

**245** **Which tribes travel and trade across the Sahara desert?**
   a) Sioux  b) Bedouin  c) Cossacks

**246** Which river runs through the middle of Paris?

a) Seine    b) Thames    c) Tiber

**247** Only female chickens lay eggs.
True or false?

**248** Who was the first man to reach the South Pole:
Roald Amundsen **or** Roald Dahl?

**249** Whose tomb was found in The Valley of the Kings?

a) Julius Caesar
b) Tutankhamun
c) Solomon

**250** Which organs clean your blood?
a) heart and kidneys
b) liver and kidneys
c) brain and liver

**251** What's the name of the space marine in *Toy Story*?
a) Stan Starman
b) Rocket Tex
c) Buzz Lightyear

**252** Which 16th-century playwright wrote *Romeo and Juliet*?

**253** Put these ages in order, oldest first:
a) Iron Age   b) Stone Age   c) Bronze Age

**254** Which part of your body do spitting cobras target: eyes **or** mouth?

**255** When knights charge at each other with wooden lances, they are:
   a) sparring    b) sniping    c) jousting

**256** Which expensive food is made entirely from fish eggs?
   a) caviar    b) blini    c) borscht

**257** Where is blood made?
   a) bones    b) heart    c) lungs

**258** Which city has over 10,000 yellow cabs?
   a) Paris    b) London    c) New York

**259** Who were tricked into taking a hollow wooden horse filled with enemy soldiers into their city?

a) the Celts
b) the Trojans
c) the Romans

**260** Which country has the most wolves?

a) Canada
b) Russia
c) United States

**261** Who were the Japanese warriors that fought with long, curved swords?

a) samurai   b) geishas   c) jedi

**262** My friend is Dr. Watson, and my enemy is the Napoleon of crime. I live at 221b Baker Street.

Who am I?

**263** Were the people of Pompeii wiped out by:

the Black Death plague **or** a volcano named Vesuvius?

**264** For most of the 20th century, which of these was the world's largest state?

a) USSR
b) USA
c) China

**265** Which waves do doctors use to see people's bones?

a) ultraviolet rays
b) gamma rays
c) X-rays

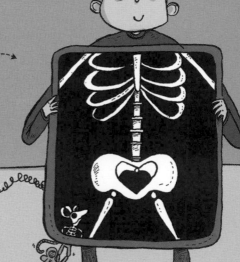

**266** Which river separates Mexico from the United States?

a) Rio Grande
b) Amazon
c) Missouri

**267** What's the name of the ghostly natural lights that sometimes billow over Scandinavia's far north?

N _ _ _ _ _ _ n L _ _ _ _ s

**268** Who was a child gangster?
a) Percy Jackson
b) Bugsy Malone
c) Draco Malfoy

**269** Put these civilizations in time order, oldest first:
a) Aztec   b) Spartan   c) Byzantine

**270** Is Mardi Gras:

a carnival with dancing and music **or** a round the world yacht race?

**271** What do fish breathe through:
nostrils **or** gills?

**272** A cannon ball and a tennis ball are dropped from a tower at the same time. What happens next?

a) the cannon ball hits the ground first
b) the tennis ball hits the ground first
c) they both hit the ground at the same time

**273** Which animal makes honey?

a) hummingbird    b) brown bear    c) bee

**274** I am the son of a goddess...
...and the greatest warrior of the Trojan War. My one weak spot is my heel.
Who am I?

**275** Where can you swim in the Blue Lagoon, heated by a volcano?

a) Iceland
b) Ireland
c) Israel

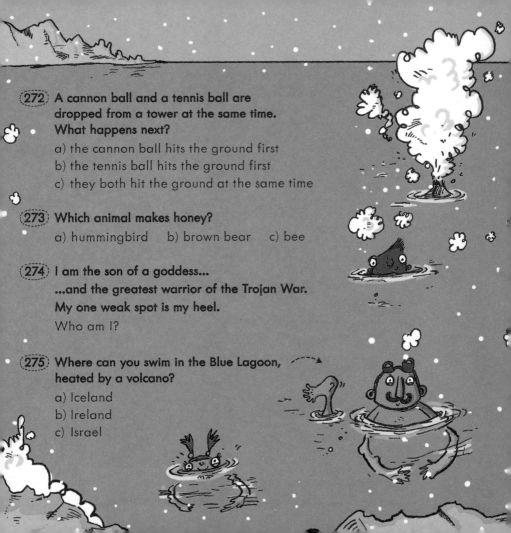

**276** Which ship was found abandoned and drifting in the ocean, with no sign of damage and no sign of her crew?

a) Mary Celeste    b) Bismarck    c) Mayflower

**277** How do you say 'goodbye' in Japanese?

a) konnichiwa    b) sayonara    c) saru

**278** Which of these was a real prehistoric animal?

a) giant koala
b) flying ostrich
c) woolly rhino

**279** Whose grandmother was eaten by a wolf?

a) Goldilocks
b) Snow White
c) Little Red Riding Hood

**280** Where can you see religious dancers known as 'whirling dervishes'?
a) Mexico
b) Turkey
c) Russia

**281** I was raised by apes in the jungle, and beat my chest as I swing through the trees. I have a wife named Jane.
Who am I?

**282** Which statement about carrots is true: they help you see in the dark **or** they can turn you orange?

**283** The first dinosaurs lived:
a) 250 years ago
b) 250 thousand years ago
c) 250 million years ago

**284** What do koalas eat?
a) bamboo
b) pampas
c) eucalyptus

**285** Complete the name of this American outlaw:

J _ _ _ _   J _ _ _ _

**286** What's the moral of the story about 'the boy who cried wolf'?
a) don't lie
b) don't steal
c) don't be selfish

**287** Which is NOT in Egypt?
a) Sphinx
b) Stonehenge
c) Pyramids of Giza

**288** Who was imprisoned by the Pope for suggesting the Earth moves around the Sun?
a) Galileo
b) Confucius
c) Plato

**289** Which basketball team did Michael Jordan play for?
a) Boston Celtics
b) Chicago Bulls
c) Los Angeles Lakers

**290** What are prehistoric flying reptiles called?
a) pterosaurs
b) stegosaurs
c) sauropods

**291** In the *Wind in the Willows*, what is Mr. Toad disguised as when he escapes from prison?
a) a washerwoman
b) a postman
c) a nurse

**292** Where do people traditionally dance flamenco?
a) Georgia
b) Cuba
c) Spain

**293** What is glass made from?
a) salt
b) sand
c) plastic

**294** What was Florence Nightingale's nickname:
The Lady with the Limp
**or** The Lady with the Lamp?

**295** Where was printing invented?
a) England    b) China    c) Italy

**296** Which Italian city is the birthplace of pizza?
a) Naples    b) Milan    c) Pisa

**297** Where in Eastern Europe can you visit a 700 year-old
salt mine with sculptures, chambers and an entire
chapel carved out of salt?
a) Greenland
b) Finland
c) Poland

**298** What are the summer storms that provide 80% of India's yearly rainfall:

cyclones **or** monsoons?

**299** The tiny coqui frog is as loud as a:
a) doorbell
b) fire alarm
c) ship's horn

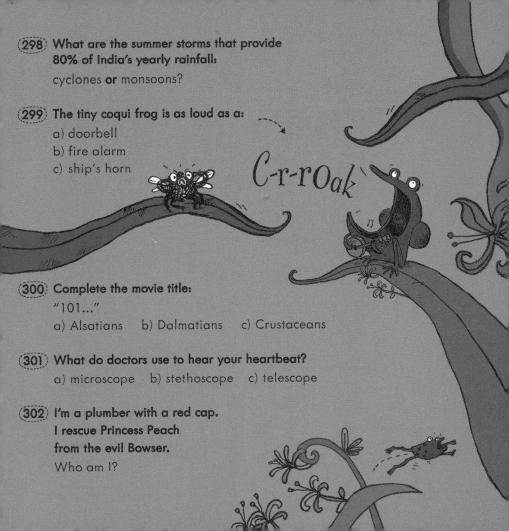

*C-r-rOak*

**300** Complete the movie title:
"101..."
a) Alsatians    b) Dalmatians    c) Crustaceans

**301** What do doctors use to hear your heartbeat?
a) microscope    b) stethoscope    c) telescope

**302** I'm a plumber with a red cap.
I rescue Princess Peach
from the evil Bowser.
Who am I?

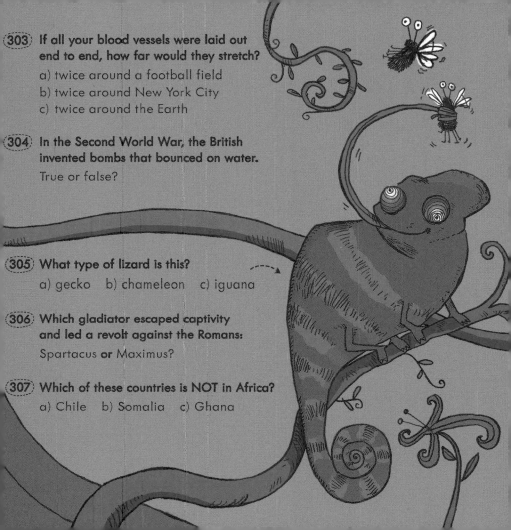

**303** If all your blood vessels were laid out end to end, how far would they stretch?
a) twice around a football field
b) twice around New York City
c) twice around the Earth

**304** In the Second World War, the British invented bombs that bounced on water.
True or false?

**305** What type of lizard is this?
a) gecko   b) chameleon   c) iguana

**306** Which gladiator escaped captivity and led a revolt against the Romans:
Spartacus **or** Maximus?

**307** Which of these countries is NOT in Africa?
a) Chile   b) Somalia   c) Ghana

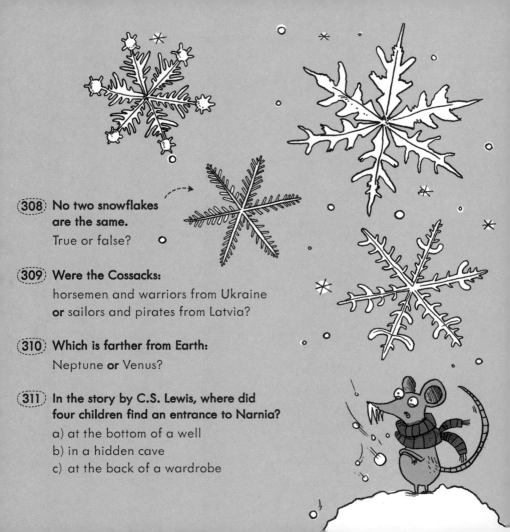

**308** No two snowflakes are the same.
True or false?

**309** Were the Cossacks:
horsemen and warriors from Ukraine
**or** sailors and pirates from Latvia?

**310** Which is farther from Earth:
Neptune **or** Venus?

**311** In the story by C.S. Lewis, where did
four children find an entrance to Narnia?
a) at the bottom of a well
b) in a hidden cave
c) at the back of a wardrobe

**312** Which animals use sonar to find their way around?

a) snails     b) crabs     c) bats

**313** Which country's flag has a white background with a red circle in the middle?

a) Japan     b) France     c) Canada

**314** Did cavemen hunt dinosaurs?

**315** Norway's coast has thousands of narrow, steep-sided inlets. What are they called:

estuaries **or** fjords?

**316** In China, are dragons said to bring good or bad luck?

**317** Jellyfish have no brain.
True or false?

**318** In the story by J.M. Barrie, what directions does Peter Pan give to Neverland? "Second star to the right, and..."
a) a left at the lights
b) a hop, a skip and a jump
c) straight on till morning

**319** Which is the smallest planet in the Solar System?

a) Mercury    b) Mars    c) Saturn

**320** Which president was assassinated in Dallas: Richard Nixon **or** John F. Kennedy?

**321** How long can a camel go without drinking?

a) 4 days    b) 4 weeks    c) 4 months

**322** Where can you see people playing steel pans and wearing Rasta hats?

a) Hawaii
b) Jamaica
c) Fiji

**323** Eskimos have over 50 words for snow. True or false?

**324** When British cities were bombed in the Second World War, it was called...
a) the Blitz
b) the Panzer
c) the Stuka

**325** What is the middle part of an atom called?
a) chromosome
b) nucleus
c) heart

**326** Which mountain was the home of the Greek gods:
Mount Sinai **or** Mount Olympus?

**327** What's the fastest bird that's ever lived?
a) peregrine falcon     b) vulture     c) golden eagle

**328** In the legends, what was Robin Hood's main weapon?
  a) pistol    b) bow and arrow    c) sword

**329** In 2007, sharks killed one human. How many sharks did humans kill in the same year?
  a) 1 million    b) 10 million    c) 100 million

**330** What's the capital of Greece?
  a) Madrid    b) Athens    c) Istanbul

$$\frac{8\pi G}{c^4}T$$

$$E = mc^2$$

**331** In what sport is a Fosbury Flop performed?
  a) gymnastics
  b) high jump
  c) diving

**332** Who is this famous physicist?

**333** Which is a cause of global warming?
a) the lighthouse effect
b) the doghouse effect
c) the greenhouse effect

**334** A blue whale's heart is the same size as a:
a) beachball     b) washing machine     c) car

**335** Whose dead body has been on display in Moscow's Red Square since 1924:
Vladimir Lenin **or** Che Guevara?

**336** What was the name of the monster that Beowulf killed?
a) Hagrid     b) Grendel     c) Smaug

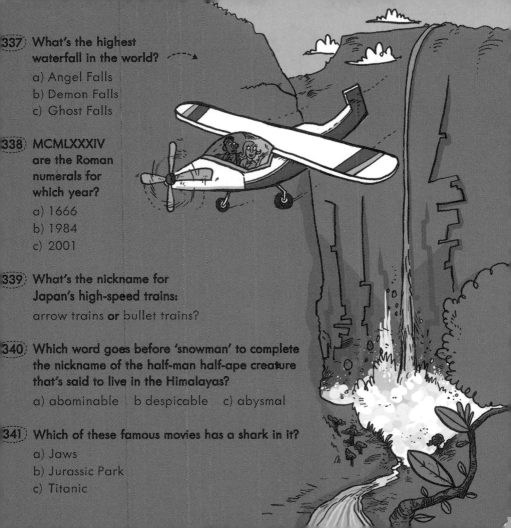

**337** What's the highest waterfall in the world?
   a) Angel Falls
   b) Demon Falls
   c) Ghost Falls

**338** MCMLXXXIV are the Roman numerals for which year?
   a) 1666
   b) 1984
   c) 2001

**339** What's the nickname for Japan's high-speed trains:
   arrow trains **or** bullet trains?

**340** Which word goes before 'snowman' to complete the nickname of the half-man half-ape creature that's said to live in the Himalayas?
   a) abominable   b despicable   c) abysmal

**341** Which of these famous movies has a shark in it?
   a) Jaws
   b) Jurassic Park
   c) Titanic

**342** In ancient Egypt, only women were turned into mummies.

True or false?

**343** Roughly how much blood is in your body?

a) 1 pint    b) 8 pints    c) 42 pints

**344** What is Morocco's capital city?

a) Casablanca

b) Cairo

c) Cardiff

**345** Which English king had six wives?

a) Charles I

b) George III

c) Henry VIII

**346** What was the name of the bear
in *The Jungle Book*?

a) Baloo    b) Baboo    c) Bagoo

**347** Put these golf scores in order,
from best to worst:

a) birdie    b) bogey    c) eagle    d) par

**348** On average, which pole is colder:
the North Pole **or** the South Pole?

**349** Which small fish from the Amazon river
can bite your finger off with one snip?

a) swordfish
b) electric eel
c) piranha

**350** We always see the same side of the Moon in the night sky.
True or false?

**351** Which planes defended Britain from invasion in the Second World War?
a) Messerschmitt 109
b) Spitfire
c) F16

**352** Which is the largest lizard in the world:
Gila monster **or** Komodo dragon?

**353** In the legend, which instrument did the Pied Piper play to entice all the rats and children away?
a) fiddle       b) flute       c) harp

**354** When the Aztecs performed a human sacrifice, what was ripped from the still-living victim and held up to the sun?

a) tongue    b) eyes    c) heart

**355** Match the animal to its description:

a) tiger    1) herbivore
b) bear    2) carnivore
c) sheep    3) omnivore

**356** Which is a popular beach in Sydney, Australia?

a) Barbie beach
b) Bondi Beach
c) Bonza Beach

**357** Where were the artists Michelangelo, Raphael and Leonardo da Vinci all born?

a) France    b) Spain    c) Italy

**358** Complete the name of the story with a peg-legged pirate called Long John Silver, and a parrot named Captain Flint.

T _ _ _ _ _ _ _    I _ _ _ _ _

**359** In the city of Montreal in Canada, how are you most likely to be greeted?

a) hello    b) bonjour    c) hola

**360** Which Australian outlaw wore a homemade metal suit to protect himself:

'Mad' Dan Morgan
or Ned Kelly?

PING

PING

**361** When did cavemen hunt woolly mammoths?

a) Bronze Age    b) Stone Age    c) Iron Age

**362** Which blood cells attack germs:

white blood cells or red blood cells?

**363** Which of these could you NOT see in the forests of eastern Russia?
a) tigers   b) bears   c) gorillas   d) wolves

**364** Which dinosaurs were usually faster:
meat-eaters **or** plant-eaters?

**365** Can astronauts float in space because:
there's more gravity **or** less gravity?

**366** What made the strange stone columns
of the Giant's Causeway in Northern Ireland?
a) volcanic eruption
b) tidal wave
c) hurricane

367) **What's the name of this desert animal that has huge ears and hops like a kangaroo?**

a) prairie dog    b) hamster    c) jerboa

368) **What do some people think Area 51 is hiding?**

a) dinosaurs    b) UFOs    c) Elvis

369) **Rasputin was an adviser to the last emperor of Russia. What was his nickname?**

a) the mad monk
b) the vicious vicar
c) the pickled priest

370) **Who invented the world wide web?**

a) Stephen Hawking
b) Tim Berners Lee
c) Bill Gates

**371** In *His Dark Materials*, who was friends with a warrior bear, a witch queen and the lord of the gyptians?

    a) Lyra    b) Bella    c) Hermione

**372** In Spain, a worried-looking man cries: "¡Mi toro se ha escapado!" What's he saying?

My watch has been stolen! **or** My bull has escaped!

**373** Which area in the Atlantic Ocean have ships sailed into and never been seen again?

    a) the Jamaica Circle
    b) the Bermuda Triangle
    c) the Haiti Square

**374** Do scorpions sting with their tail, their pincers or both?

**375** The Ashes cricket series has been contested for over 100 years between Australia and which country?

    a) West Indies    b) South Africa    c) England

**376** Which cartoon character says 'What's up, Doc?'
a) Daffy Duck
b) Mickey Mouse
c) Bugs Bunny

**377** A crusade to capture Jerusalem was led by Richard the...
a) Tigerclaw    b) Lionheart    c) Squirreltail

**378** Does a banana have DNA?

**379** Not all dinosaurs were huge.
These Compsognathuses were the size of...
a) mice
b) chickens
c) kangaroos

**380** Which movie hero went to the ancient Middle Eastern city of Petra to find the Holy Grail?

a) Indiana Jones
b) Luke Skywalker
c) Lara Croft

**381** Which sport has a quarterback?

a) American football
b) rugby
c) basketball

**382** What is Santa Claus' name in Russia: Papa Midnight or Grandfather Frost?

**383** What is the world's most venomous animal?

a) black widow spider
b) box jellyfish
c) king cobra

**384** On which date in 1776 did America declare independence from Great Britain?

a) February 14
b) July 4
c) October 31

**385** **Where can you lie back and read a magazine without sinking?**
   a) Sea of Galilee
   b) Red Sea
   c) Dead Sea

**386** **In the very first Olympic Games, which was NOT an event?**
   a) archery
   b) a race in full battledress
   c) naked wrestling

**387** **Roughly how many dust mites live in your bed?**
   a) 25      b) 2,500      c) 25,000

**388** **What is the name of the Simpsons' pet dog?**
   a) Snowball
   b) Santa's Little Helper
   c) Stompy

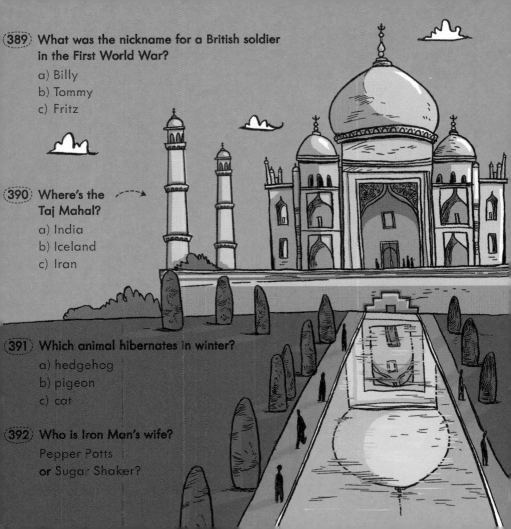

**389** What was the nickname for a British soldier in the First World War?
a) Billy
b) Tommy
c) Fritz

**390** Where's the Taj Mahal?
a) India
b) Iceland
c) Iran

**391** Which animal hibernates in winter?
a) hedgehog
b) pigeon
c) cat

**392** Who is Iron Man's wife?
Pepper Potts
**or** Sugar Shaker?

**393** Which mythical character had snakes for hair?

a) Medusa    b) Minotaur    c) Cerberus

**394** What did Winnie the Pooh and Piglet try to trap in a deep hole with a jar of honey?

a) a womble    b) a moomin    c) a heffalump

**395** What's the name for the eagle standard (banner) that all Roman legions carried into battle:

aquila **or** aqueduct?

**396** Does the Sun:

spin around **or** stay still?

**397** Sailors on long voyages used to suffer from a deadly disease called scurvy. Which food could prevent it:

lemons **or** cheese?

**398** What's the name for a dog that's a cross between a poodle and a labrador?

a) poodledor    b) labrapoo    c) labradoodle

**399** What's the world's longest railway, which runs across all of Russia?

a) Trans-Arabian Railway
b) Trans-Bavarian Railway
c) Trans-Siberian Railway

**400** If a Mexican calls to you "Hey, gringo!" what's he saying?

a) Hey, foreigner!
b) Hey, fancy pants!
c) Hey, friend!

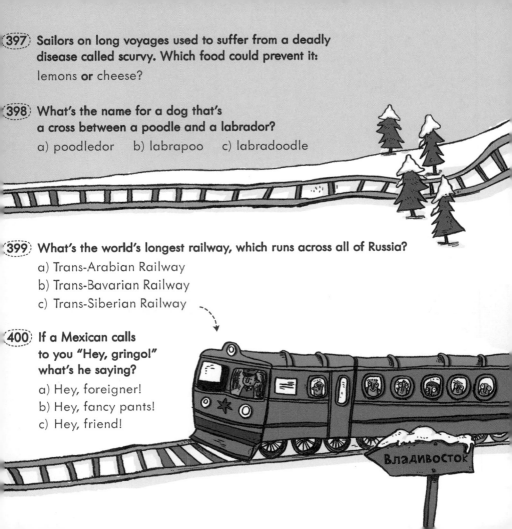

Владивосток

**401** Who first discovered North America:
the Vikings **or** the Chinese?

**402** What is a group of small islands called?
a) archipelago
b) estuary
c) lagoon

**403** During the First World War, officers sometimes received messages by homing pigeon.
Could they send the pigeons back with a reply?

**404** Put these animals in the order they went extinct:
a) woolly mammoth
b) Tyrannosaurus rex
c) dodo

**405** Where is it rude to finish all your dinner, because it indicates that your host hasn't given you enough to eat?
a) China
b) Scotland
c) Iran

**406** Is carbon dioxide a solid, a liquid or a gas?

**407** I have two big orange teeth...
...and a talent for felling trees.
I'm also Canada's national animal.
What am I?

**408** Who were the Second World War pilots who
deliberately flew their planes into enemy battleships?
a) kamikaze pilots
b) banzai pilots
c) shogun pilots

**409** What's this huge canyon in the United States called?

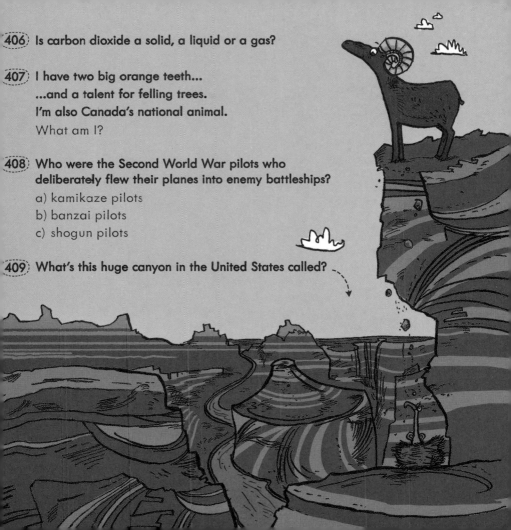

**410** Only male stegosaurs had plates on their backs?

True or false?

**411** What did Hansel and Gretel find in the woods?

a) seven dwarfs
b) a gingerbread house
c) a big bad wolf

**412** Which creature is on the Welsh national flag?

a) unicorn   b) dragon   c) griffin

**413** How many bacteria live in your body?

a) none
b) one hundred
c) one hundred trillion

**414** Where's Death Valley, the world's hottest desert?
   a) Australia
   b) Saudi Arabia
   c) United States

**415** The word 'dinosaur' means:
   a) ancient lizard
   b) terrible lizard
   c) giant lizard

**416** Octopuses squirt ink to drive away predators.
   True or false?

**417** Who shot Mr. Burns in *The Simpsons*?
   a) Groundskeeper Willie
   b) The Comic Book Guy
   c) Maggie Simpson

**418** Noodles grow on trees.
   True or false?

**419** What did stegosaurs eat?
a) meat   b) fish   c) plants

**420** Which legendary city is said to be lost underwater?
a) Avalon   b) Atlantis   c) Shangri-La

**421** When you're dehydrated you feel:
a) thirsty
b) hungry
c) tired

**422** Roughly how many times do cows pass gas each day?
a) 15   b) 150   c)1,500

**423** If you flew from Tokyo to London on New Year's Eve, would New Year come earlier or later than if you'd stayed in Japan?

**424** In which stadium is the FA Cup Final played?
a) Old Trafford    b) Wembley    c) Anfield

**425** How many hours do koalas sleep a day?
a) 5 hours    b) 10 hours    c) 20 hours

**426** Stick insects are made of wood.
True or false?

**427** Where was the US naval base that was
attacked by Japan in the Second World War?
a) Pearl Harbor    b) Ruby Harbor    c) Emerald Harbor

**428** Which character in Moominvalley leaves a trail of ice
and freezes the ground wherever she sits?
a) the Hemulen    b) the Groke    c) Little My

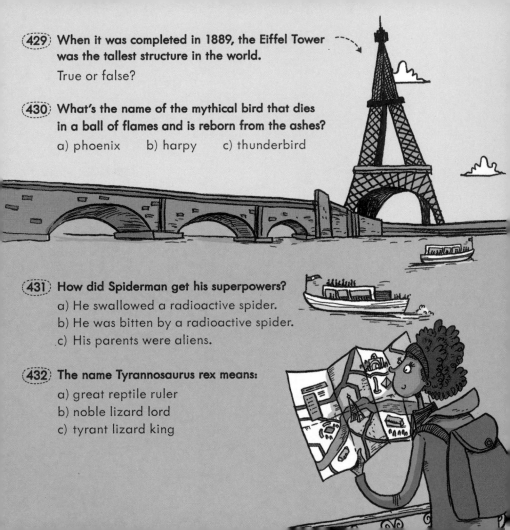

**429** When it was completed in 1889, the Eiffel Tower was the tallest structure in the world.

True or false?

**430** What's the name of the mythical bird that dies in a ball of flames and is reborn from the ashes?

a) phoenix    b) harpy    c) thunderbird

**431** How did Spiderman get his superpowers?

a) He swallowed a radioactive spider.
b) He was bitten by a radioactive spider.
c) His parents were aliens.

**432** The name Tyrannosaurus rex means:

a) great reptile ruler
b) noble lizard lord
c) tyrant lizard king

**433** Who burned down Washington DC in 1814?

a) the British    b) the French    c) the Russians

**434** What are you supposedly given when you kiss the Blarney Stone in Ireland?

a) fabulous riches
b) the gift of the gab
c) eternal youth

**435** What is this scientist looking through?

a) miniscope
b) microscope
c) macroscope

**436** What was inside Aladdin's lamp?

a) a genie
b) a goblin
c) a dragon

**437** What do matadors use in bullfights?

   a) black cape    b) blue cape    c) red cape

**438** At the 2012 Olympic Games held in London,
who won gold in both the 100m and 200m?

   a) Maurice Greene
   b) Usain Bolt
   c) Yohan Blake

**439** 'Timbuktu' is the name for what?

   a) a species of monkey
   b) a type of mango
   c) a town in Mali

**440** Which award can a movie win?

   a) a Bertie    b) a Winston    c) an Oscar

**441** A blue whale can blow its spout as high as a:

   a) 1-floor building
   b) 3-floor building
   c) 6-floor building

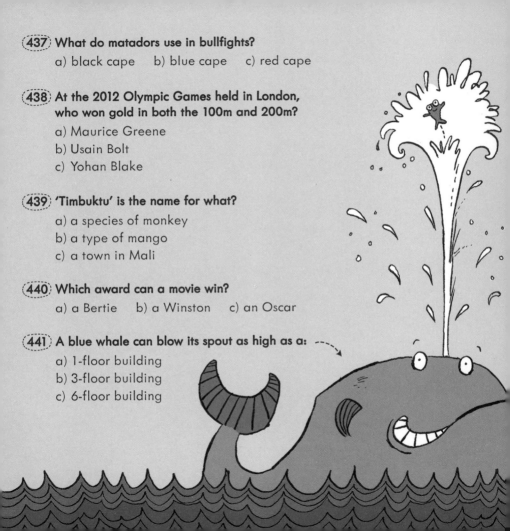

**442** In the legends, which wizard helped King Arthur?

a) Merlin    b) Gandalf    c) Harry Potter

**443** If you were cast adrift in space without a spacesuit, you'd explode.

True or false?

**444** Where would a Tyrannosaurus rex be most at home today?

a) the deserts of northern Africa
b) the mountains of the Himalayas
c) the swamps of Florida

**445** Who is NOT a famous scientist?

a) Charles Dickens
b) Charles Darwin
c) Stephen Hawking

**446** While looking after its egg, how long does an emperor penguin go without food?

a) 2 days    b) 2 weeks    c) 2 months

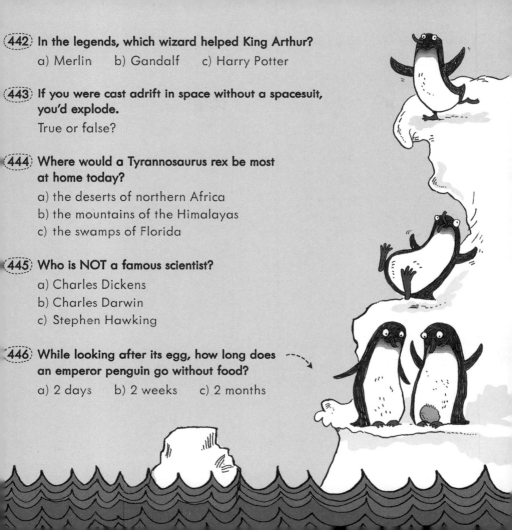

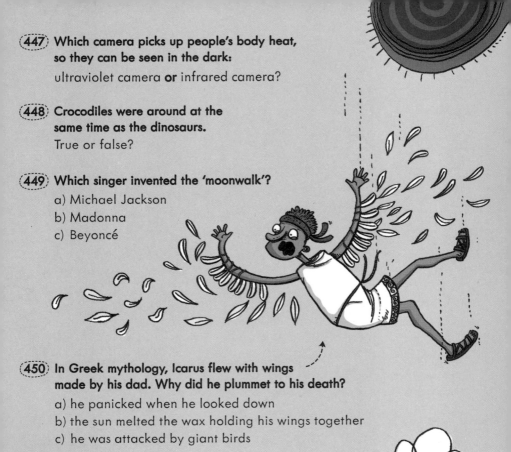

**447** Which camera picks up people's body heat, so they can be seen in the dark:

ultraviolet camera **or** infrared camera?

**448** Crocodiles were around at the same time as the dinosaurs.
True or false?

**449** Which singer invented the 'moonwalk'?
a) Michael Jackson
b) Madonna
c) Beyoncé

**450** In Greek mythology, Icarus flew with wings made by his dad. Why did he plummet to his death?
a) he panicked when he looked down
b) the sun melted the wax holding his wings together
c) he was attacked by giant birds

**451** Which is NOT a real place?
a) Transylvania    b) Zanzibar    c) Valhalla

**452** Who is a famous golfer?

a) Bear Woods    b) Eagle Woods    c) Tiger Woods

**453** I was a fearsome horseback warrior from Mongolia...

...and the most successful conqueror of all time.

One of my grandsons was Kublai Khan.

Who am I?

**454** Which ancient civilization lived
deep in the rainforest?

a) the Celts

b) the Apache

c) the Mayans

**455** Does a proboscis monkey have:

a) a giant nose?

b) a fat belly?

c) a huge moustache?

**456** Which food doesn't grow on trees?

a) bananas    b) carrots    c) lemons

**457** A marketplace in North Africa is called a...

a) bazaar    b) farrago    c) gumbo

**458** Which rocket took astronauts to the Moon for the first time?

a) Apollo 1    b) Apollo 11    c) Apollo 13

**459** Who is NOT one of Batman's enemies?

a) Bane    b) Lex Luthor    c) The Penguin

**460** In the Middle Ages, who used potions to search for the Philosopher's Stone and the Elixir of Life?

a) alchemists    b) crusaders    c) priests

**461** Who was the first cricketer to score one hundred international centuries and is nicknamed 'The Little Master'?

a) Viv Richards    b) Shane Warne    c) Sachin Tendulkar

**462** I'm from the hot grasslands in Africa.
I have a tassel on the end of my tail.
I'm known as the king of the beasts.
What am I?

**463** Who's called the 'father of science' because he studied everything around him so closely?

a) Julius Caesar
b) Marco Polo
c) Aristotle

**464** Which toy was invented in Denmark?

a) Lego
b) yo-yo
c) Rubik's cube

**465** Who built the Acropolis?

    a) Romans    b) Saxons    c) ancient Greeks

**466** In the Harry Potter books, what's the name of Harry's owl?

    a) Scabbers    b) Hedwig    c) Pig

**467** Which is elastic?

    a) rubber    b) wood    c) glass

**468** Which animal is nicknamed 'the old man of the forest'?

    a) orangutan
    b) parrot
    c) alligator

**469** What does a human brain feel like?

a) soft-boiled egg    b) milk    c) apple

**470** Which country sold Alaska to the United States in 1867?

a) Mexico    b) Russia    c) Australia

**471** What is a baby kangaroo called?

a) bunny    b) sheila    c) joey

**472** What type of dancing can you see at the Rio Carnival in Brazil?

a) foxtrot
b) tango
c) samba

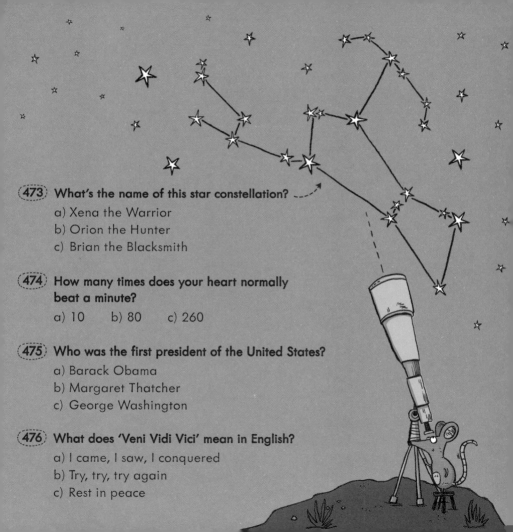

**473** What's the name of this star constellation?
a) Xena the Warrior
b) Orion the Hunter
c) Brian the Blacksmith

**474** How many times does your heart normally beat a minute?
a) 10    b) 80    c) 260

**475** Who was the first president of the United States?
a) Barack Obama
b) Margaret Thatcher
c) George Washington

**476** What does 'Veni Vidi Vici' mean in English?
a) I came, I saw, I conquered
b) Try, try, try again
c) Rest in peace

**477** Which team has David Beckham NOT played for?
a) Manchester United
b) Arsenal
c) Real Madrid

**478** What part of an elephant's body has over 100,000 muscles but no bones?

**479** What is Japan's nickname?
a) Land of the Rising Sun
b) Land of the Yellow Moon
c) Land of the Long Grass

**480** What scientific discovery was inspired by an apple falling from a tree?
a) magnetism
b) evolution
c) gravity

**481** In the comic books, who was a member of the X-Men?
a) The Joker
b) Storm
c) Doctor Octopus

**482** If you're on the beach in Italy and someone says to you:
"I tuoi piedi odorano di formaggio", what are they saying?

a) The water's very warm.
b) Your feet smell of cheese.
c) I've got sand in my trunks.

**483** People catch chickenpox from eating chicken.
True or false?

**484** What type of animal is a bat?

a) mammal
b) reptile
c) bird

**485** What was invented first:
fire **or** the wheel?

**486** Is the 15th Century from:

a) 1401–1500
b) 1500–1599
c) 1501–1600

**487** Which country has borders with China, the United States, Finland and Ukraine?

a) Russia    b) Canada    c) India

**488** Which storybook hero said: "Please, sir, I want some more."

a) Huckleberry Finn
b) Oliver Twist
c) Peter Pan

**489** What are the remains of this old dinosaur called?

a) fossil    b) corpse    c) embryo

**490** I pricked my finger on a spinning wheel, and fell asleep for one hundred years. I was woken by a prince's kiss.

Who am I?

**491** What sport do Roger Federer and Serena Williams play?

a) basketball    b) tennis    c) golf

**492** Why did a Stegosaurus and a Tyrannosaurus rex never fight each other?
   a) they were both plant-eaters
   b) they were scared of each other
   c) they lived at different times

**493** What can you watch in Spain: bullfights **or** gladiator fights?

**494** Which disease can you catch from mosquitoes?
   a) malaria
   b) pneumonia
   c) tuberculosis

**495** Who is Luke Skywalker's mentor in *Star Wars*?
   a) Obi-Wan Kenobi
   b) Boba Fett
   c) Jabba the Hutt

**496** What legendary ghost ship is condemned to sail the seas for all eternity?
a) The Dawn Treader
b) The Flying Dutchman
c) The Golden Hind

**497** I have eight legs.
I have large pincers and I sting with my tail.
My deadliest species is called 'deathstalker'.
What am I?

**498** What is the chemical symbol for water:
NaCl or $H_2O$?

**499** What's the opposite of northwest?

**500** Who took part in the gunfight at the OK Corral?
a) Jesse James
b) Billy the Kid
c) Wyatt Earp

**501** What's the highest mountain in the world?

a) Kilimanjaro   b) Mont Blanc   c) Everest

**502** Which can you see from the International Space Station:

the Pyramids of Giza **or** the Great Wall of China?

**503** Which of Doctor Who's enemies only moves when you're not looking?

a) the Cybermen
b) the Silence
c) the Weeping Angels

**504** What does cold air give you?

a) dogbumps
b) goosebumps
c) bunnybumps

505) Which African animal eats ants, and can somersault away from trouble?

a) hippo    b) aardvark    c) wildebeest

506) Dracula is based on which historic prince, who executed his enemies on wooden stakes?

a) Vlad the Impaler    b) Grisha the Gorer    c) Bram the Staker

507) The ancient Greeks did calculations on:

a) an abacus    b) a calculator    c) a xylophone

508) I'm a metal that's liquid at room temperature. I share my name with a small planet... ...and a Roman god.

What's my name?

509) Which jersey does the leading rider in the Tour de France cycle race wear?

a) red jersey    b) yellow jersey    c) blue jersey

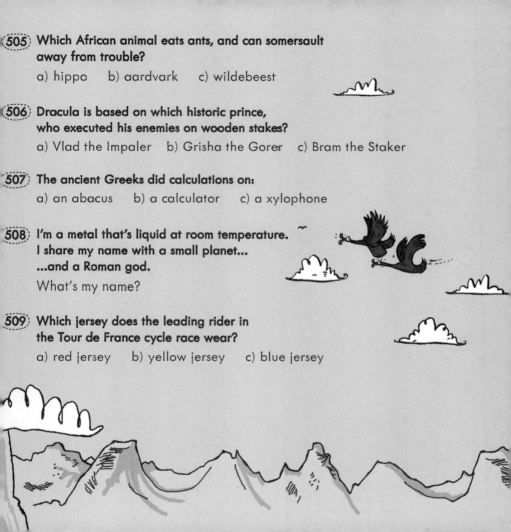

**510** What's often used by fishermen as bait?

a) maggots
b) frogs
c) cheese

**511** Who led the first expedition to sail around the world, but died on the way?

Ferdinand Magellan **or** Christopher Columbus?

**512** Which country gave the Statue of Liberty as a present to the United States?

a) Britain      b) Russia      c) France

**513** Which would win in a fight between a great white shark and a killer whale?

**514** In what sport can you take part in a scrum, smash into other players and score a try?

a) ice hockey     b) wrestling     c) rugby

**515** Which of these was one of Henry VIII's six wives:

Anne Boleyn **or** Anne Hathaway?

**516** Which is NOT a chemical element?

a) mucus     b) sodium     c) copper

**517** The hardest thing a Triceratops could chew through was a:

a) leaf
b) tree trunk
c) rock

**518** Which of these ancient Greeks never existed?

a) Achilles
b) Socrates
c) Homer

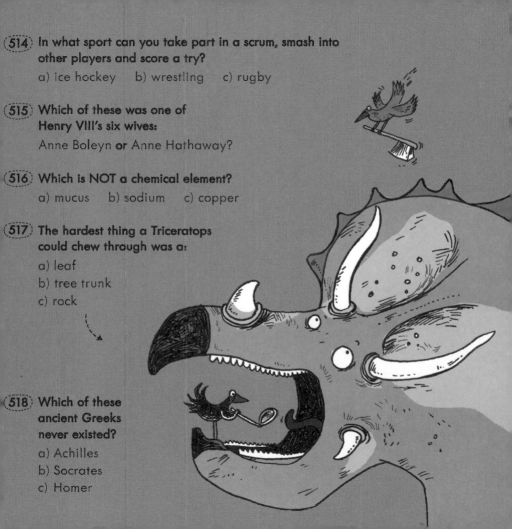

519) **Which sheep was the first ever cloned mammal?**
a) Polly      b) Dolly      c) Molly

520) **What is Pisa famous for?**
a) a leaning tower
b) an upside-down statue
c) a bottomless well

521) **What was the name of the ship that took the Pilgrim Fathers to America?**
M _ _ f _ _ _ _ _

522) **Who stole the three bears' porridge?**
a) Goldilocks      b) Coraline      c) Snow White

**523** I have only one foot to move around on.
I have eyes on long, thin stalks.
I carry my home on my back.
What am I?

**524** What's the ring of water around a castle called?
a) keep    b) knave    c) moat

**525** Which driver holds the record for winning the most Formula One world championships?
a) Michael Schumacher    b) Ayrton Senna    c) Lewis Hamilton

**526** Where do fishermen use trained birds to catch fish?
a) England
b) Turkey
c) China

# Answers

**1.** c

**2.** c

**3.** b

**4.** false (It was painted by Leonardo da Vinci.)

**5.** a

**6.** c (The stench drives away disease-ridden parasites.)

**7.** a

**8.** b

**9.** c

**10.** a

**11.** Orville & Wilbur Wright (The first flight took place in 1903.)

**12.** The Nile

**13.** b

**14.** c

**15.** a

**16.** a (Cats are more adaptable than dogs, because they don't need as much attention or space.)

**17.** b

**18.** a

**19.** b

**20.** c

**21.** b

**22.** b

**23.** a2 b3 c1

**24.** c

**25.** c

**26.** a

**27.** b

**28.** c

**29.** a

**30.** b (Because it contains calcium.)

**31.** c

**32.** c

**33.** no (There are no air particles to carry the sound.)

**34.** b (They hadn't evolved yet.)

**35.** c

**36.** c

**37.** a (Rhinos follow their ears more than their eyes.)

**38.** b

**39.** a

**40.** b

**41.** a (Its first manned flight was in 1783.)

**42.** c

**43.** c

**44.** Vikings

**45.** a

**46.** c

**47.** a

**48.** b

**49.** Nelson Mandela

**50.** vinegar

**51.** a

**52.** c

**53.** c

**54.** a

**55.** b

**56.** grizzly bears (A grizzly bear can break a lion's skull with one swipe.)

**57.** a

**58.** a

**59.** Colditz

**60.** a

**61.** c

**62.** a

**63.** a

**64.** c

**65.** b

**66.** b, c and e

**67.** false (It had the head of a bull.)

**68.** Jupiter

**69.** b

**70.** b

**71.** b

**72.** c

**73.** a
**74.** c (Some historians think this story is a myth.)
**75.** Portuguese
**76.** b
**77.** a
**78.** c
**79.** false (They store fat there.)
**80.** *Titanic*
**81.** c
**82.** true
**83.** a
**84.** the Sun
**85.** a
**86.** a
**87.** b
**88.** a
**89.** c
**90.** a (In *The Wizard of Oz*, by L. Frank Baum.)
**91.** Blackbeard the pirate
**92.** b
**93.** mistletoe
**94.** false
**95.** c
**96.** a
**97.** Joan of Arc
**98.** c
**99.** viruses
**100.** c

**101.** no (Polar bears live near the North Pole and penguins live near the South Pole.)
**102.** b
**103.** uranium
**104.** five times smaller
**105.** a
**106.** a3 b1 c2
**107.** b
**108.** false
**109.** b
**110.** a
**111.** the Lost City of Gold (In Spanish, 'el dorado' means 'golden one'. There was a local tribe whose kings used to cover themselves in gold dust, then sail out into a sacred lake to offer treasures to their goddess. The legend grew from this, and local people would get rid of European explorers by saying the lost city of gold was "over there" in the distance.)
**112.** a
**113.** mane
**114.** c

**115.** one (These camels are called dromedaries. Camels with two humps are called bactrians.)
**116.** c
**117.** c (The Dakar Rally is an off-road motor race.)
**118.** c
**119.** a
**120.** a (The far east of Russia nearly reaches the western tip of Alaska.)
**121.** leeches (In the Middle Ages, medics believed many illnesses could be cured by draining blood; so they often used blood-sucking leeches in their treatments.)
**122.** b (It's the only one that isn't a country.)
**123.** c
**124.** c
**125.** false (It might be possible, in theory, over a long period of time, to breed a dinosaur species back into existence. But scientists have never found enough dinosaur

DNA to attempt it.)
**126.** b
**127.** false (Water can spiral down a drain in either direction, anywhere in the world.)
**128.** a
**129.** b
**130.** c
**131.** c (He was born on the planet Krypton.)
**132.** false (Your lungs collect oxygen from the air you breathe in.)
**133.** c
**134.** yes (A passenger jet is struck by lightning about once a year, but is designed to withstand the strike.)
**135.** an owl
**136.** b (standard can size – 414g / 15oz.)
**137.** c (It carries deadly diseases.)
**138.** a3 b1 c2
**139.** c
**140.** b (He was Pharaoh of ancient Egypt from 1333-1323BC.)
**141.** a

**142.** Amelia Earhart
**143.** Triceratops
**144.** b
**145.** below it (Icebergs are floating in the sea: only the top part sticks out above the water.)
**146.** b
**147.** a
**148.** c
**149.** no (He's a legendary figure, probably based on a variety of people.)
**150.** a (Sidewinding is the easiest way for a snake to move across sand.)
**151.** b
**152.** the Moon (It's because of the Moon's gravitational attraction. As the Moon orbits the Earth, the water below is pulled towards it.)
**153.** b
**154.** Vietnam War
**155.** b
**156.** b
**157.** c
**158.** c
**159.** Wallace

**160.** Rome
**161.** b
**162.** a
**163.** false
**164.** a
**165.** c
**166.** salty seadog
**167.** c
**168.** c
**169.** b
**170.** c
**171.** a (In *James and the Giant Peach,* by Roald Dahl.)
**172.** a
**173.** b
**174.** b
**175.** a
**176.** c
**177.** c (Most mammals evolved after the dinosaurs had died out.)
**178.** b
**179.** a
**180.** true
**181.** a
**182.** c
**183.** the Jolly Roger
**184.** Mary Poppins
**185.** b
**186.** b

**187.** a

**188.** c (Some dinosaurs are very closely related to modern birds. In fact, many scientists believe that birds are the direct descendants of dinosaurs.)

**189.** a

**190.** true

**191.** a

**192.** a

**193.** separately

**194.** c

**195.** a

**196.** c

**197.** West coast

**198.** tortoise

**199.** b

**200.** c

**201.** a

**202.** c

**203.** b

**204.** b

**205.** Muhammad Ali

**206.** plesiosaur

**207.** c

**208.** Tyrannosaurus rex

**209.** c

**210.** c

**211.** Pinocchio

**212.** b

**213.** a (He was from the former Soviet Union, and blasted into space on April 12, 1961.)

**214.** b

**215.** Antoni Gaudí (It's called the Sagrada Família and is famous for its strange stonework, which seems to have grown from the ground like a living thing.)

**216.** King Arthur (In the legend, he was the only person who could pull the sword from the stone, proving he was the true king of England.)

**217.** smaller

**218.** pirates

**219.** b

**220.** c

**221.** a

**222.** no (Only mammals have bellybuttons.)

**223.** a

**224.** Gandhi

**225.** b

**226.** a

**227.** Great Wall of China

**228.** General Custer

**229.** c

**230.** c (There's a star for each American state.)

**231.** b

**232.** a

**233.** b (Blue whales are larger than even the largest dinosaur.)

**234.** a black hole

**235.** c

**236.** James Bond

**237.** Julius Caesar

**238.** b

**239.** Robinson Crusoe

**240.** b

**241.** llama

**242.** b (He flew the spaceship by pulling levers when they lit up.)

**243.** a

**244.** b (Magma is liquid rock. When it erupts, it's called lava.)

**245.** b

**246.** a

**247.** true

**248.** Roald Amundsen (Roald Dahl was named after him.)

**249.** b (See note to question 140.)

**250.** b

**251.** c

**252.** William Shakespeare

**253.** b c a

**254.** eyes

**255.** c

**256.** a

**257.** a

**258.** c

**259.** b (Greek soldiers were hiding inside.)

**260.** a (Followed by Russia.)

**261.** a

**262.** Sherlock Holmes

**263.** a volcano named Vesuvius

**264.** a

**265.** c

**266.** a

**267.** Northern Lights

**268.** b

**269.** b c a

**270.** a carnival with dancing and music

**271.** gills

**272.** c (The force of gravity is the same for all objects.)

**273.** c

**274.** Achilles (a mythical hero of ancient Greece)

**275.** a

**276.** a

**277.** b

**278.** c

**279.** c

**280.** b

**281.** Tarzan

**282.** they can turn you orange (The myth about carrots helping you see in the dark was spread by British intelligence in the Second World War, because they didn't want the enemy to know they'd invented a radar system.)

**283.** c

**284.** c

**285.** Jesse James

**286.** a

**287.** b (It's in England.)

**288.** a

**289.** b

**290.** a

**291.** a

**292.** c

**293.** b

**294.** The Lady with the Lamp

**295.** b

**296.** a

**297.** c

**298.** monsoons

**299.** b

**300.** b

**301.** b

**302.** Mario

**303.** c (And an adult's would stretch four times around the Earth.)

**304.** true (They were built to destroy dams, by bouncing along the surface of the water and exploding when they hit the dam wall.)

**305.** b

**306.** Spartacus

**307.** a (It's in South America.)

**308.** true (Although occasionally tiny snow crystals fall from the sky. These haven't yet grown into snowflakes, and look very similar to each other.)

**309.** horsemen and warriors from Ukraine

**310.** Neptune

**311.** c

**312.** c

**313.** a

**314.** no (Dinosaurs died out long before cavemen were around.)

**315.** fjords

**316.** good luck

**317.** true

**318.** c (That's the line from the Disney film. In the original play it's "second to the right and then straight on till morning".)

**319.** a

**321.** John F. Kennedy

**321.** b

**322.** b

**323.** false (Eskimo has about the same number of words for snow as English. But the Sami people, who live in the far north of the Nordic countries, have about 300 words for snow.)

**324.** a

**325.** b

**326.** Mount Olympus

**327.** a (It reaches 320kph (200mph) when diving after prey.)

**328.** b

**329.** c

**330.** b

**331.** b

**332.** Albert Einstein

**333.** c

**334.** c

**335.** Vladimir Lenin (He was the leader of the Russian Revolution in 1917.)

**336.** b

**337.** a

**338.** b

**339.** bullet trains

**340.** a

**341.** a

**342.** false

**343.** b

**344.** a

**345.** c

**346.** a

**347.** c a d b

**348.** South Pole (The South Pole is in Antarctica, which is the highest continent in the world because the ground is covered by a sheet of ice so thick it swallows up mountains. It's this extra height that makes the South Pole colder than the North Pole.)

**349.** c

**350.** true

**351.** b

**352.** Komodo dragon

**353.** b

**354.** c

**355.** a2 b3 c1

**356.** b

**357.** c

**358.** Treasure Island

**359.** b (Montreal is a mainly French-speaking city.)

**360.** Ned Kelly

**361.** b

**362.** white blood cells

**363.** c

**364.** meat-eaters

**365.** less gravity (There's gravity everywhere, but the farther you are from a big object (such as a planet) the less there is.)

**366.** a

**367.** c

**368.** b (In 1947 a UFO is said to have landed in

Roswell, New Mexico, and been taken to Area 51 – a remote US Air Force base in the Nevada desert. Until 2013 all research and events at Area 51 were classified as top secret, which increased its air of mystery.)

**369.** a

**370.** b

**371.** a

**372.** My bull has escaped!

**373.** b

**374.** tail

**375.** c

**376.** c

**377.** b (It was called the Third Crusade, and aimed to recapture Jerusalem from Saladin.)

**378.** yes (All living things contain DNA (Deoxyribonucleic acid).)

**379.** b

**380.** a (Petra was called 'The Temple of the Sun' in the movie.)

**381.** a

**382.** Grandfather Frost

**383.** b (A box jellyfish sting can kill you in three minutes.)

**384.** b

**385.** c (The Dead Sea is so thick with salt it can support a person's weight.)

**386.** a

**387.** c

**388.** b

**389.** b

**390.** a

**391.** a

**392.** Pepper Potts

**393.** a

**394.** c

**395.** aquila

**396.** spin around

**397.** lemons (This is because they contain lots of Vitamin C.)

**398.** c

**399.** c

**400.** a

**401.** the Vikings

**402.** a

**403.** no (They only fly one way – home.)

**404.** b a c

**405.** a

**406.** a gas (At room temperature.)

**407.** beaver

**408.** a

**409.** the Grand Canyon

**410.** false

**411.** b

**412.** b

**413.** c

**414.** c (Its record temperature is 56.7°C (134°F).)

**415.** b

**416.** true

**417.** c

**418.** false (They are made from flour paste.)

**419.** c

**420.** b

**421.** a

**422.** c

**423.** earlier (As you go from west to east, the time goes forward. For example, when it's 1pm in New York, it's 5pm in London.)

**424.** b

**425.** c

**426.** false

**427.** a

**428.** b

**429.** true

**430.** a

**431.** b

**432.** c

**433.** a

**434.** b

**435.** b

**436.** a

**437.** c

**438.** b

**439.** c

**440.** c

**441.** b

**442.** a

**443.** false (You'd swell up slightly, but you wouldn't explode, or freeze, and your blood wouldn't boil. You'd pass out after 30 seconds from lack of oxygen, and after that you'd die.)

**444.** c

**445.** a

**446.** c

**447.** infrared camera (Also called a thermal imaging camera, it detects infrared energy. The hotter something is, the more infrared energy it gives off.)

**448.** true

**449.** a

**450.** b

**451.** c (Transylvania is an area of Romania, in Eastern Europe. Zanzibar is a group of islands off the coast of Tanzania that used to be a haunt for slave traders and pirates. Valhalla is a mythical hall for Viking warriors who died in battle.)

**452.** c

**453.** Genghis Khan

**454.** c

**455.** a

**456.** b

**457.** a

**458.** b

**459.** b

**460.** a

**461.** c

**462.** a lion

**463.** c

**464.** a

**465.** c

**466.** b

**467.** a

**468.** a

**469.** a

**470.** b (The United States bought it for the bargain price of 2 cents per acre.)

**471.** c

**472.** c

**473.** b

**474.** b

**475.** c

**476.** a

**477.** b

**478.** its trunk

**479.** a

**480.** c

**481.** b

**482.** b

**483.** false (It's caught from contact with an infected person.)

**484.** a

**485.** fire

**486.** a

**487.** a

**488.** b (In the book *Oliver Twist,* by Charles Dickens.)

**489.** a

**490.** Sleeping Beauty

**491.** b

**492.** c (The Stegosaurus

lived 152 million years ago, and the T. rex lived 65 million years ago. On the timeline of life on Earth, the T. rex is closer to humans than it is to the Stegosaurus!)

**493.** bullfights
**494.** a
**495.** a
**496.** b
**497.** a scorpion
**498.** $H_2O$
**499.** southeast
**500.** c
**501.** c (It's 8,848m (9,676 yds) high.)
**502.** the Pyramids of Giza (The Pyramids are quite easy to spot because they're wide and cast big shadows. The Great Wall of China is virtually impossible to see from space because it's thin and blends in with the surrounding ground.)

**503.** c
**504.** b
**505.** b
**506.** a
**507.** a
**508.** Mercury
**509.** b
**510.** a
**511.** Ferdinand Magellan (He died in the Philippines in 1521, about two thirds of the way through his 'round the world' voyage.)
**512.** c (The statue was built in France and shipped to America in 1885.)
**513.** a killer whale (It's much bigger and more intelligent.)
**514.** c
**515.** Anne Boleyn
**516.** a
**517.** b
**518.** a (He was a hero of Greek myth, although he may have been based

partly on real people.)
**519.** b
**520.** a
**521.** *Mayflower*
**522.** a
**523.** a snail
**524.** c
**525.** a
**526.** c

## Cover questions

**Did all dinosaurs eat meat?** No (Most dinosaurs ate plants – including the one on the cover, called a Mamenchisaurus.)

**Who was the first man on the moon?** Neil Armstrong

**Can lions purr?** No (Lions, tigers, jaguars and leopards can't purr.)

**Where is the Grand Canyon?** Arizona in the United States

Digital manipulation by Keith Furnival

First published in 2014 by Usborne Publishing Ltd. 83–85 Saffron Hill, London ECIN 8RT, England. Copyright ©2014 Usborne Publishing Ltd. The name Usborne and the devices ♈ ⊕ are Trade Marks of Usborne Publishing Ltd. All rights reserved. No part of this publication may be reproduced, stored in a retrieval system, or transmitted in any form or by any means, electronic, mechanical, photocopying, recording or otherwise, without the prior permission of the publisher. First published in America in 2014. UE. Printed in Shenzen, Guangdong, China.